DAILY SENTENCE STRETCHERS

# DAILY SENTENCE STRETCHERS

| How to Use Daily Sentence Stretchers | pages 2-4 |
| --- | --- |
| Primary Sentence Stretchers | pages 5-30 |
| Advanced Sentence Stretchers | pages 31-56 |
| Blank Sentence Stretchers | pages 57-60 |
| About the Author | page 61 |
| MediaStream Press | page 62 |

## COPYRIGHT & OTHER NOTES

All material and designs in this book are copyrighted (C) 2016 Andrew Frinkle. Graphics and cliparts are from openclipart.org or other royalty free sources.

You may make copies of the material within the book for personal and classroom use only. This is a single-teacher/user license.

It is suggested that you check the prompts you will use before using them with your children or students. Please remove any that you do not think are appropriate for the age level of the students or the setting. They are provided to be interesting writing experiences, but may not fit for all students and situations.

(C) 2016 MediaStream Press & Andrew Frinkle

# HOW TO USE DAILY SENTENCE STRETCHERS

Each page is designed for use over several days, but they could be done all on one day, or with partners and small groups.

Starting Sentence

A sentence box per day. Add to the previous, OR start each one with the starter sentence and modify according to your dice rolls.

Record what you rolled each day in the blank dice boxes. Use numbers or draw the dots on the dice.

Roll dice each day. Use these options to stretch your sentences. You can cross out one as you use it to get more variety in your writing.

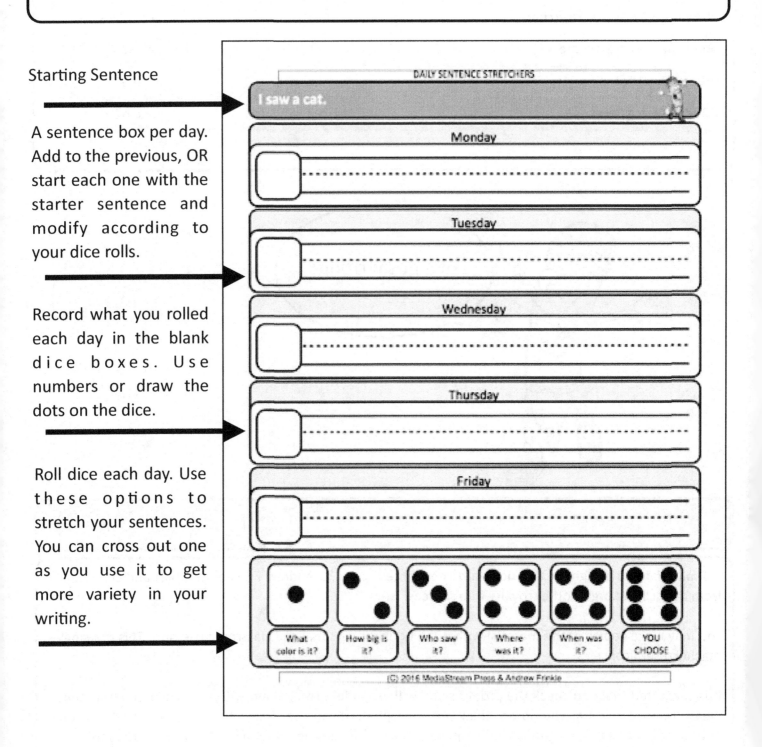

DAILY SENTENCE STRETCHERS

## I saw a cat. (EXAMPLE - RESTARTING EACH SENTENCE)

### Monday
 I saw a black cat.

### Tuesday
 I saw a Siamese cat.

### Wednesday
 I saw a cat under the bushes.

### Thursday
 I saw a cat yesterday.

### Friday
 Jim and I saw a cat.

 color
 size
 location
 type
 who?
 when?

(C) 2016 MediaStream Press & Andrew Frinkle

DAILY SENTENCE STRETCHERS

## I saw a cat. (EXAMPLE - CONTINUING EACH SENTENCE)

### Monday

I saw a black cat.

### Tuesday

I saw a black, Siamese cat.

### Wednesday

I saw a black, Siamese cat under the bushes.

### Thursday

I saw a black, Siamese cat under the bushes yesterday.

### Friday

Jim and I saw a black, Siamese cat under the bushes yesterday.

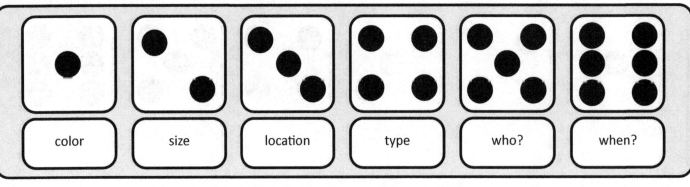

(C) 2016 MediaStream Press & Andrew Frinkle

DAILY SENTENCE STRETCHERS

# PRIMARY SENTENCE STRETCHERS

Practice writing sentences with beginning writers.
Add description and detail to basic sentences.

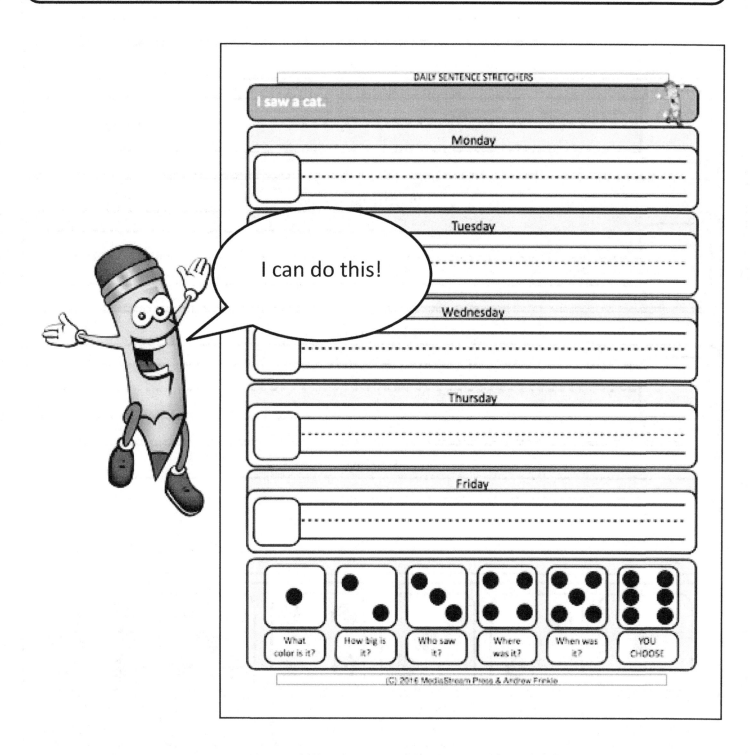

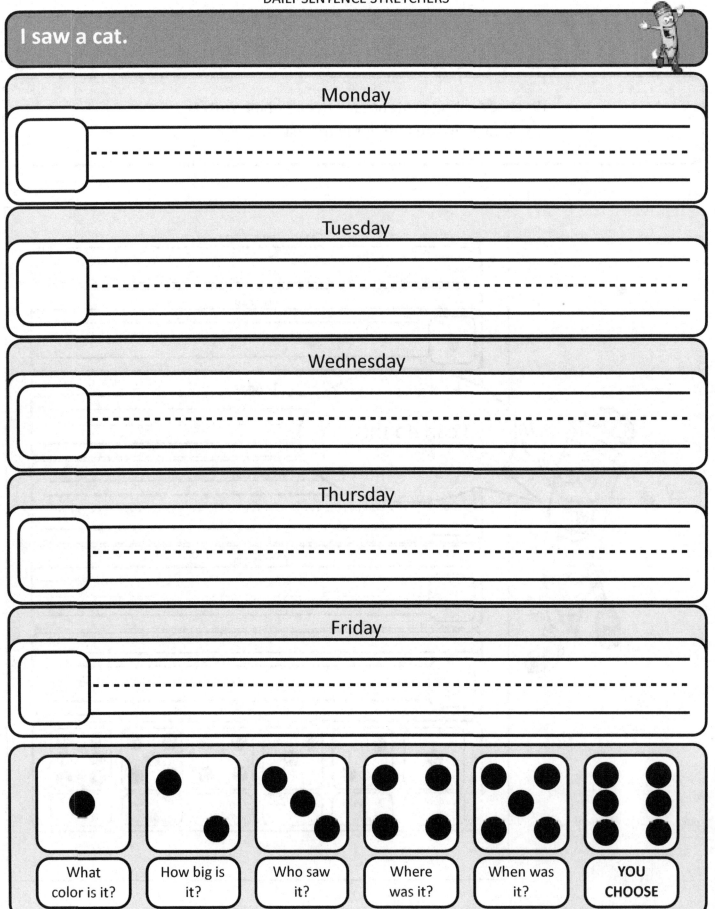

DAILY SENTENCE STRETCHERS

**I have a coat.**

Monday

Tuesday

Wednesday

Thursday

Friday

| What color is it? | How big is it? | What kind is it? | Why? | Add an adjective | YOU CHOOSE |

DAILY SENTENCE STRETCHERS

## I have a sticker collection.

### Monday

### Tuesday

### Wednesday

### Thursday

### Friday

| Where is it? | How big is it? | Why do you have it? | Who gave it to you? | Add an adjective | YOU CHOOSE |

DAILY SENTENCE STRETCHERS

# I ate candy.

## Monday

## Tuesday

## Wednesday

## Thursday

## Friday

| What color? | What kind? | What flavor? | How much? | When did you eat it? | YOU CHOOSE |

DAILY SENTENCE STRETCHERS

## I went to the store.

### Monday

### Tuesday

### Wednesday

### Thursday

### Friday

| Who went with you? | Which store? | Where is it? | Why did you go? | When did you go? | YOU CHOOSE |

DAILY SENTENCE STRETCHERS

## We had a party.

### Monday

### Tuesday

### Wednesday

### Thursday

### Friday

| Who was there? | What kind of party? | Where was it? | When was it? | Add an adjective | YOU CHOOSE |

DAILY SENTENCE STRETCHERS

## I watched a movie.

### Monday

### Tuesday

### Wednesday

### Thursday

### Friday

| When? | Who was with you? | Where? | What did you eat? | Which movie? | YOU CHOOSE |

## DAILY SENTENCE STRETCHERS

**He climbed a tree.**

### Monday

### Tuesday

### Wednesday

### Thursday

### Friday

| What kind? | How high? | How fast? | Where was it? | Change tense | YOU CHOOSE |

DAILY SENTENCE STRETCHERS

## There is a fish.

### Monday

### Tuesday

### Wednesday

### Thursday

### Friday

| What color? | What kind of fish? | Where is it? | What size is it? | What is it doing? | YOU CHOOSE |

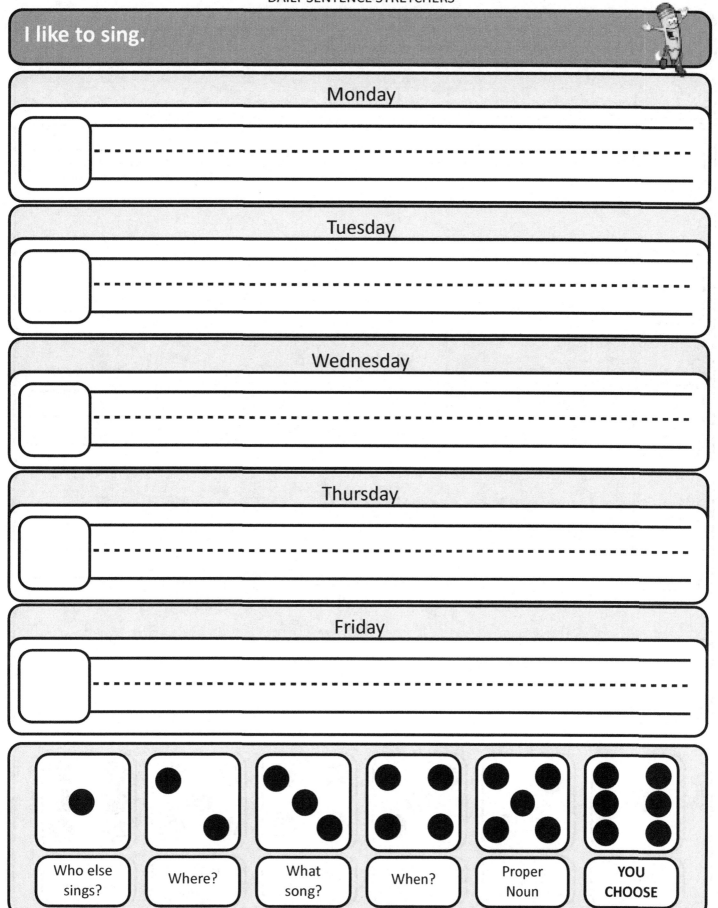

DAILY SENTENCE STRETCHERS

## Yesterday, I went to school.

### Monday

### Tuesday

### Wednesday

### Thursday

### Friday

| When? | Why? | How? | Where? | Proper Noun | YOU CHOOSE |

# DAILY SENTENCE STRETCHERS

## Please give me the glue.

### Monday

### Tuesday

### Wednesday

### Thursday

### Friday

| Change subject | Change object | When? | Verb Synonym | Add an adjective | YOU CHOOSE |

DAILY SENTENCE STRETCHERS

## "Hello." Sara said to me.

### Monday

### Tuesday

### Wednesday

### Thursday

### Friday

| Change pronoun | Change greeting | When? | Where? | Verb Synonym | YOU CHOOSE |

(C) 2016 MediaStream Press & Andrew Frinkle

# DAILY SENTENCE STRETCHERS

## I ate a cookie.

### Monday

### Tuesday

### Wednesday

### Thursday

### Friday

| Plural noun | Change pronoun | Proper Noun | Verb Synonym | Add an adjective | YOU CHOOSE |

# Where is my hat?

## Monday

## Tuesday

## Wednesday

## Thursday

## Friday

| Change pronoun | Change object | Past tense | Proper Noun | Add an adjective | YOU CHOOSE |

# DAILY SENTENCE STRETCHERS

## Look at me.

### Monday

### Tuesday

### Wednesday

### Thursday

### Friday

| Change pronoun | Verb Synonym | Proper Noun | When? | Change to question | YOU CHOOSE |

DAILY SENTENCE STRETCHERS

**I read a book.**

## Monday

## Tuesday

## Wednesday

## Thursday

## Friday

| 1 | 2 | 3 | 4 | 5 | 6 |
|---|---|---|---|---|---|
| What kind of book? | When? | How fast? | Change verb | Add an adjective | YOU CHOOSE |

(C) 2016 MediaStream Press & Andrew Frinkle

DAILY SENTENCE STRETCHERS

## The birds were flying.

### Monday

### Tuesday

### Wednesday

### Thursday

### Friday

| Change to singular | What kind of bird? | Where? | When? | Change verb | YOU CHOOSE |

(C) 2016 MediaStream Press & Andrew Frinkle

DAILY SENTENCE STRETCHERS

**Tom bought a cake.**

## Monday

## Tuesday

## Wednesday

## Thursday

## Friday

| Plural subject | Plural object | Where? | When? | Add an adjective | YOU CHOOSE |

(C) 2016 MediaStream Press & Andrew Frinkle

DAILY SENTENCE STRETCHERS

**Ryan put on his shoes.**

Monday

Tuesday

Wednesday

Thursday

Friday

| When? | Where? | Why? | Change to pronoun | Add an adjective | YOU CHOOSE |

(C) 2016 MediaStream Press & Andrew Frinkle

DAILY SENTENCE STRETCHERS

## I walk to school.

### Monday

### Tuesday

### Wednesday

### Thursday

### Friday

| -ing verb form | Past tense | Future tense | When? | Proper noun | YOU CHOOSE |

DAILY SENTENCE STRETCHERS

## We played a game.

### Monday

### Tuesday

### Wednesday

### Thursday

### Friday

| What game? | Proper nouns | When? | Where? | Add an adjective | YOU CHOOSE |

(C) 2016 MediaStream Press & Andrew Frinkle

DAILY SENTENCE STRETCHERS

## Sing a song for me.

### Monday

### Tuesday

### Wednesday

### Thursday

### Friday

| Change the verb | Make it a question | When? | Change pronoun | Add an adjective | YOU CHOOSE |

DAILY SENTENCE STRETCHERS

## Do you like that?

### Monday

### Tuesday

### Wednesday

### Thursday

### Friday

| Make it a statement | Change object | Change subject | Add an adverb | Proper Noun | YOU CHOOSE |

DAILY SENTENCE STRETCHERS

## Jamie has a pony.

### Monday

### Tuesday

### Wednesday

### Thursday

### Friday

| adjective | preposition | pronoun | conjunction | change tense | YOU CHOOSE |

DAILY SENTENCE STRETCHERS

## ADVANCED SENTENCE STRETCHERS

Practice writing sentences with advanced writers.
Use those parts of speech and punctuation marks!

(C) 2016 MediaStream Press & Andrew Frinkle

DAILY SENTENCE STRETCHERS

## He ate a(n) _____ .

### Monday

### Tuesday

### Wednesday

### Thursday

### Friday

| color | size | when? | flavor | who? | YOU CHOOSE |

# DAILY SENTENCE STRETCHERS

## He rode a _____.

### Monday

### Tuesday

### Wednesday

### Thursday

### Friday

| adjective | preposition | adverb | conjunction | compound subject | YOU CHOOSE |

# DAILY SENTENCE STRETCHERS

## I saw a _____.

### Monday

### Tuesday

### Wednesday

### Thursday

### Friday

| , | ! | ? | ; | ( ) | YOU CHOOSE |

# DAILY SENTENCE STRETCHERS

## She can _____ .

### Monday

### Tuesday

### Wednesday

### Thursday

### Friday

| adverb | preposition | adjective | conjunction | use a synonym | YOU CHOOSE |

# I lost my _____ .

## Monday

## Tuesday

## Wednesday

## Thursday

## Friday

| in | on | under | behind | after | YOU CHOOSE |

DAILY SENTENCE STRETCHERS

## Can you see the _____ ?

### Monday

### Tuesday

### Wednesday

### Thursday

### Friday

| color | size | conjunction | compound object | proper noun | YOU CHOOSE |

DAILY SENTENCE STRETCHERS

## He took my _____ .

### Monday

### Tuesday

### Wednesday

### Thursday

### Friday

| conjunction | adjective | adverb | preposition | proper noun | YOU CHOOSE |

DAILY SENTENCE STRETCHERS

**I can't wait for _____ .**

Monday

Tuesday

Wednesday

Thursday

Friday

| conjunction | adjective | adverb | preposition | compound subject | YOU CHOOSE |

DAILY SENTENCE STRETCHERS

**The dog chased the _____ .**

## Monday

## Tuesday

## Wednesday

## Thursday

## Friday

| conjunction | adjective | adverb | preposition | use a synonym | YOU CHOOSE |

DAILY SENTENCE STRETCHERS

**I wish I could _____ .**

### Monday

### Tuesday

### Wednesday

### Thursday

### Friday

| conjunction | adjective | adverb | preposition | change to a question | YOU CHOOSE |

DAILY SENTENCE STRETCHERS

**She climbed a _____ .**

## Monday

## Tuesday

## Wednesday

## Thursday

## Friday

| Future Tense | Present Tense | adverb | preposition | adjective | YOU CHOOSE |

DAILY SENTENCE STRETCHERS

## Look at that _____ !

### Monday

### Tuesday

### Wednesday

### Thursday

### Friday

| preposition | adjective | when? | change to a statement | change to a question | YOU CHOOSE |

# DAILY SENTENCE STRETCHERS

**Will you cook some _____ for dinner?**

## Monday

## Tuesday

## Wednesday

## Thursday

## Friday

| conjunction | adjective | change tense | change occasion | change to a statement | YOU CHOOSE |

DAILY SENTENCE STRETCHERS

## When can we _____ ?

### Monday

### Tuesday

### Wednesday

### Thursday

### Friday

| conjunction | adjective | preposition | change subject | change to a statement | YOU CHOOSE |

# DAILY SENTENCE STRETCHERS

## I really hate _____ !

### Monday

### Tuesday

### Wednesday

### Thursday

### Friday

| conjunction | adjective | adverb | preposition | change to a question | YOU CHOOSE |

DAILY SENTENCE STRETCHERS

## Where is the _____ ?

### Monday

### Tuesday

### Wednesday

### Thursday

### Friday

| conjunction | adjective | preposition | interjection | change to a statement | YOU CHOOSE |

# DAILY SENTENCE STRETCHERS

## _____ are the best pet.

### Monday

### Tuesday

### Wednesday

### Thursday

### Friday

| conjunction | adjective | adverb | preposition | change to a question | YOU CHOOSE |

DAILY SENTENCE STRETCHERS

## When does _____ start?

### Monday

### Tuesday

### Wednesday

### Thursday

### Friday

| conjunction | adjective | adverb | preposition | change to a statement | YOU CHOOSE |

DAILY SENTENCE STRETCHERS

## I caught a _____ .

### Monday

### Tuesday

### Wednesday

### Thursday

### Friday

| why? | when? | where? | how? | who? | YOU CHOOSE |

## DAILY SENTENCE STRETCHERS

**Give _____ to me.**

### Monday

### Tuesday

### Wednesday

### Thursday

### Friday

| change pronoun | adjective | when? | change to exclamation | change to a question | YOU CHOOSE |

DAILY SENTENCE STRETCHERS

## Do you want to build a _____ ?

### Monday

### Tuesday

### Wednesday

### Thursday

### Friday

| conjunction | adjective | adverb | preposition | change to a statement | YOU CHOOSE |

DAILY SENTENCE STRETCHERS

# I can't believe you just _____ !

## Monday

## Tuesday

## Wednesday

## Thursday

## Friday

| change pronouns | preposition | adverb | change tenses | change to a question | YOU CHOOSE |

DAILY SENTENCE STRETCHERS

## I cried, because _____ .

### Monday

### Tuesday

### Wednesday

### Thursday

### Friday

| change subject | proper noun | change conjunction | preposition | change to a question | YOU CHOOSE |

DAILY SENTENCE STRETCHERS

The _____ costs _____ dollars.

## Monday

## Tuesday

## Wednesday

## Thursday

## Friday

| compound subject | adjective | use a synonym | preposition | change to a question | YOU CHOOSE |

DAILY SENTENCE STRETCHERS

**Robert and Susan went to _____ .**

### Monday

### Tuesday

### Wednesday

### Thursday

### Friday

| pronoun | adjective | adverb | preposition | change tense | YOU CHOOSE |

# BLANK SENTENCE STRETCHERS PAGES

Make your own sentence stretchers!
Copy these blank pages and write the starting sentence and dice descriptions.

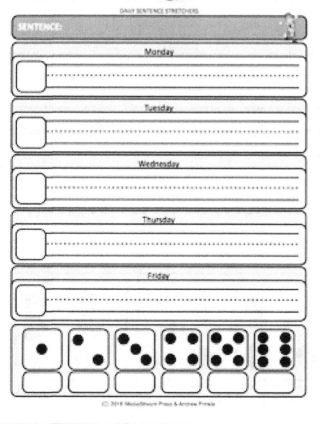
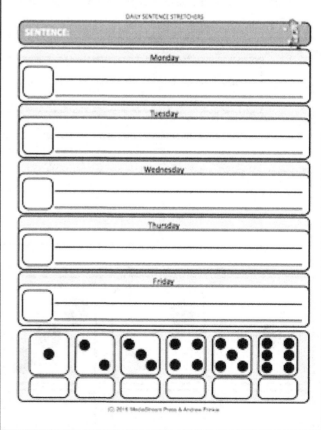

DAILY SENTENCE STRETCHERS

**SENTENCE:**

Monday

Tuesday

Wednesday

Thursday

Friday

DAILY SENTENCE STRETCHERS

**SENTENCE:**

## Monday

## Tuesday

## Wednesday

## Thursday

## Friday

DAILY SENTENCE STRETCHERS

**SENTENCE:**

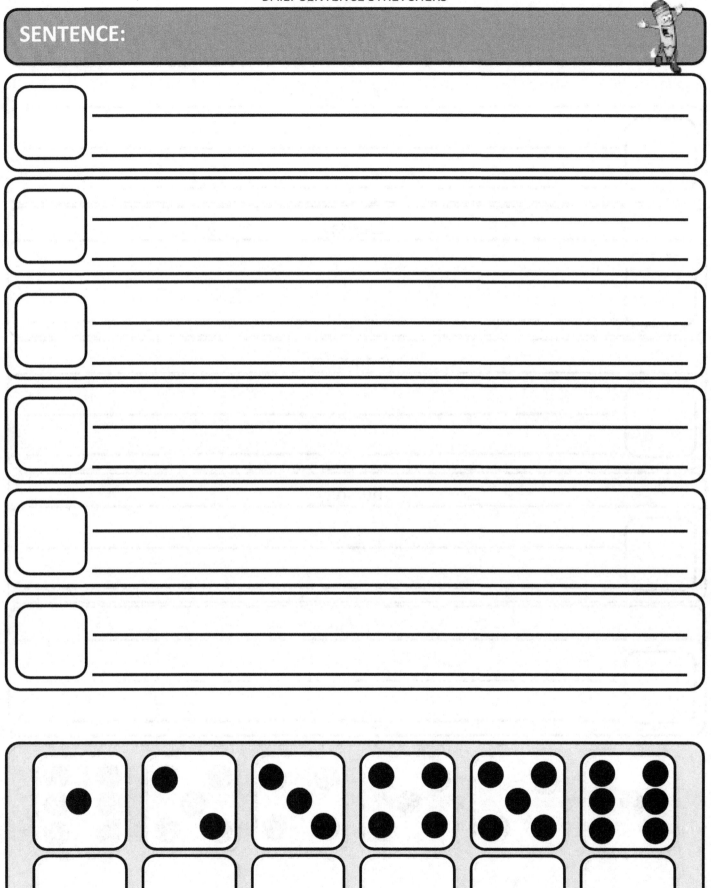

# ANDREW FRINKLE

Andrew Frinkle is an award-nominated teacher and writer with experience in America and overseas, as well as years developing educational materials for big name educational sites like Have Fun Teaching. He has taught PreK all the way up to adult classes, and has focused on ESOL/EFL techniques, as well as STEM Education. With two young children at home now, he's been developing more and more teaching strategies and books aimed at helping young learners.

His many educational works include:
*50 STEM Labs Series: 50 STEM Labs, 50 More STEM Labs, 50 New STEM Labs, 50 STEM Labs Cards, 50 STEM Labs Journals, & 50 Weeks of STEM Labs
*50 Learning Labs Series: 50 Science Labs, 50 Social Studies Labs, 50 Arts Labs, 50 Literacy Labs, 50 Math Labs, & 50 Custom Labs
*Elementary & Middle School Common Core Workbooks (K-8)

*Literacy Builders Series: Sentence Builders, Word Builders, Story Starters, and more!
*Movers and Shakers Card Game & Expansion Sets
*Basic Skills Workbooks: Alphabet Skills, Colors, Number Sense, Nursery Rhymes, Phonics, Shapes, and more!
*Sight Words Hopscotch Series
*Blank Comic Books Series: Manga, Comic Book, and Graphic Novel versions
*Board Game in a Book Series
*Card Game in a Book Series

Andrew Frinkle is the founder & owner of MediaStream Press LLC, which maintains the educational websites: www.littlelearninglabs.com, www.50STEMLabs.com, and www.common-core-assessments.com. He also writes fantasy and science fiction novels under the pen name Velerion Damarke. Read more at www.underspace.org

# MEDIASTREAM PRESS

MediaStream Press offers over 80 fun and innovative books and games to help educate. Learn more at: www.MediaStreamPress.com or search and buy directly at: www.amazon.com/author/andrewfrinkle.

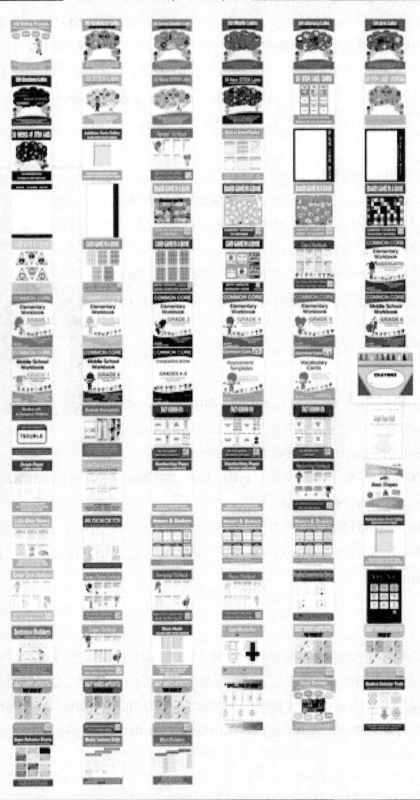

Made in the USA
Middletown, DE
20 May 2022